BRAVE COUPLES

A 30-DAY MARRIAGE NURTURING PRACTICE

By Metta Smith

Dear Jacob & Teri,
   May your love grow & flourish as you practice nurturing each other and your marriage relationship through all the seasons of your life together.
   Love & blessings, as you celebrate this special anniversary year,
         Metta & Milt

BRAVE COUPLES is a resource for couples desiring renewal and growth in their relationship. BRAVE COUPLES makes no healing claims for couples who are stuck in reactive relationship cycles or in need of healing from childhood or other past relationship trauma. However, the BRAVE COUPLES practices can serve as an adjunct to counseling for couples, who are working with a professional.

BRAVE COUPLES is available at:
CreateSpace eStore, Marriage Nurturing website and Amazon
www.amazon.com/dp/1517180287
www.amazon.ca/dp/1517180287
www.amazon.co.uk/dp/1517180287
www.createspace.com/5716684

metta.milt@marriagenurturing.org
www.MarriageNurturing.org

All revenues from book sales go to support the non-profit, Marriage Nurturing Matters.

Publisher: Metta Smith
Printed by: Create Space
ISBN-13: 978-1517180287
ISBN-10: 1517180287

Editorial Support: Judith Ryan
Cover and Interior Design: Judith Ryan
Cover and Interior Photos: Judith Ryan

Copyright © 2015, Metta Smith, all rights reserved. No part of this book may be reproduced, electronically stored, or transmitted in any form by any means, electronic, mechanical, photocopied, recorded or otherwise, without prior written permission of the author. Exceptions to the foregoing constraints are made for BRAVE COUPLES nurturing practices, which couples are encouraged to copy as worksheets.

Scriptures' quotations are taken from the HOLY BIBLE, NEW INTERNATIONAL VERSION ®. Copyright © 1973, 1978, 1984 by International Bible Society. Used by permission of Zondervan Publishing House. All rights reserved.

Dedication

To all the brave couples who are nurturing their marriages with quality time and attention, devoted to loving one another and seeking each other's best.

And now these three remain: faith, hope and love. But the greatest of these is love.

1 Corinthians 13:13

CONTENTS

Introduction 7

Getting Started 8
The power of community support.

Practice One 11
Express your love daily with *Affection and Appreciation.*

Practice Two 17
Maintain connection with Daily Check-ins.

Practice Three 21
Increase intimacy with weekly *Couple Nurturing Time.*

Finale – Share and Celebrate 31
Consider a group celebration ~ Plan a special date night.

Afterglow 33

Appendix 47

Both in counseling couples and in workshops ... I have taught people from all walks of life how to turn bad relationships into good ones, and good relationships into great ones. Because great is what you're really after. Great is what you deserve.

Not merely a relationship you can live with, but one that is truly alive --- passionately, tenderly, maddeningly filled to the brim with unexpected twists and turns, with comfort and solidity, with the sense of knowing and being known, and loving each other anyway. How do you get such a relationship? You don't get it, you build it, thoughtfully and skillfully, brick by brick.

Terrence Real, *The New Rules of Marriage*

Introduction

When my husband Milt and I married in 1962, we believed our passionate love and our vow before God — *to love honor and cherish each other for life* — was all we needed for our relationship to grow and thrive. Very soon our life grew in complexity. As it did, our passion and intense emotional connection that drew us together waned. Gradually our differences and unmet expectations led to power struggles.

It became clear that our initial commitment was not enough. We needed help. We knew we were not alone in our struggle to create closeness and harmony. Facing our disillusionment, we sought out a counselor. Slowly we changed our self-defeating beliefs and attitudes by learning skills to help us grow the love that lasts, with the intimacy we longed for.

Research bears out what we experienced. A great marriage doesn't happen naturally. From reading *Fighting for Your Marriage*, we learned that it takes two commitments; first, a commitment to taking "a long view of marriage," and second, to "make your marriage a priority." With our marriage vows secure, we said *"yes"* to a new commitment of *intentional nurturing* and *seeking each other's best*. As we nurtured each other, our relationship grew in intimacy and mutual satisfaction. It took work — at times challenging work — but our reward is the aliveness Terrance Real describes on the opposite page.

When our children were grown, rather than returning to my former work as a registered nurse, I pursued a graduate degree and became a mental health counselor. While I was in school, the seed for a class to help couples develop intimacy skills was planted. After I became licensed and established my counseling practice, I began developing *Marriage Nurturing*. It has evolved into an eight-session, interactive, small group experience ~ with "nurturing work" assigned between sessions. Over the past 15 years Milt and I have taught several hundred couples how to nurture each other, and how to develop an intimate and mutually supportive relationship.

Eighteen months ago, I awakened with an idea for a 30-day *marriage nurturing experience,* using three central practices from our *Marriage Nurturing* course. My desire was to invite couples to "taste and see" how *marriage nurturing* can enliven their love and instill fresh hope for a great future together. This idea grew into BRAVE COUPLES ~ a self-led, manageable bite for couples with busy lives.

BRAVE COUPLES gives you specific ways to invest quality time and energy into your relationship. It contains everything you need for a month of *marriage nurturing*. As you attend to each other in new ways, you can expect a reduction in conflict common to most couples.

BRAVE COUPLES includes a plan for encouragement and group support. It isn't easy to make changes and form new habits. We encourage you to find some other brave couples to join you. This will enhance your experience. Also, we know how life can take over and make it easy to "forget" your practice. So, please be gentle with yourself and your beloved if that happens, and simply return to the practices. If you have any questions, feel free to email us: metta.milt@marriagenurturing.org

With renewed joy that a deepening, intimate friendship brings, these essential practices will support and energize your love through all the seasons of life. We hope this taste of *marriage nurturing* will make you hungry for more.

Metta Smith

Getting Started with Community Support
*Consider meeting for an hour once a week with other
brave couples for encouragement and prayer.*

Our Need for Support

We are not meant to go it alone. *Lessons from Geese* remind us how much we need the support of others on our marriage journey for encouragement, strength and ongoing hope for a good future together.

Milt and I have attended a number of marriage workshops over the years. Each time we returned home inspired and believing we would put our new learning into practice. Soon our ordinary life once again took all our time and space. Alone, we couldn't sustain the energy and determination we needed for making lasting changes.

Over time we learned we needed a *flock of couples* with our same desire for a thriving intimate marriage. With regular encouragement and support, we get the *uplift* we need to keep learning and growing intimacy in all aspects of our relationship.

Lessons from Geese
From naturalist Milton Olsen as told to Angeles Arrien in a speech given at the 1991 Organizational Development Network.

FACT 1: As each goose flaps its wings, it creates "uplift" for the birds that follow. By flying in a "V" formation, the whole flock adds 71% greater flying range than if each bird flew alone.

LESSON: People who share a common direction and sense of community can get where they are going more quickly and easily because they are traveling on the thrust of one another.

FACT 2: When a goose falls out of formation, it suddenly feels the drag and resistance of flying alone. It quickly moves back into formation to take advantage of the lifting power of the bird immediately in front of it.

LESSON: If we have as much sense as a goose, we will stay in formation with those headed where we want to go. We are willing to accept their help and give our help to others.

FACT 3: When the lead goose tires, it rotates back into formation and another goose flies in the point position.

LESSON: It pays to take turns doing the hard tasks and sharing leadership. As with geese, people need each other's skills, capabilities, and unique arrangements of gifts, talents, or resources.

FACT 4: The geese flying in formation honk to encourage those up front to keep up their speed.

LESSON: We need to make sure our honking is encouraging. In groups where there is encouragement, the production is much greater.

FACT 5: When a goose gets sick, wounded, or shot down, two geese drop out of formation and follow it to help and protect it. They stay with it until it dies or is able to fly again. Then, they launch out with another formation or catch up with the flock.

LESSON: If we have as much sense as geese, we will stand by each other in difficult times as well as when we are strong.

Brave Couples Weekly Support ~ Suggested Format

Once you have identified other brave couples for your journey, here is a suggested format.

- Open with a prayer.

- Ground Rules for week one: *Appendix*, page 49

- Encourage each other.

- Share a highlight experience from this week's nurturing practices.

- Share something you are feeling challenged by this week.

- Share other concerns if present.

- Spiritual Encouragement with *Lecteo Divina ~ meditative scripture reading*
  Suggested scriptures; feel free to substitute.
    Week 1: Psalm 100
    Week 2: Colossians 3: 12-17
    Week 3: Psalm 103: 1-12
    Week 4: John 15: 4, 5, 7-11

- Discussion on a chosen topic.

- Closing prayer for each other and your marriages

- Week Four, Finale — Share and Celebrate

But when I said that nothing had been done, I erred in one important matter. We had definitely committed ourselves and were halfway out of our ruts. We had put down our passage money—booked a sailing to Bombay. This may sound too simple, but it is great in consequence.

Until one is committed, there is hesitancy, the chance to draw back, always ineffectiveness. Concerning all acts of initiative and creation, there is one elementary truth, the ignorance of which kills countless ideas and splendid plans: that the moment one definitely commits oneself, then, Providence moves too.

All sorts of things occur to help one that would never otherwise have occurred. A whole stream of events issue from the decision, raising in one's favour all manner of unforeseen incidents meetings and material assistance which no man could have dreamed would have come his way. I learned a deep respect for one of Goethe's couplets: Whatever you can do or dream you can, begin it. Boldness has genius, power, and magic in it. Begin it now.

From *The Himalayan Expedition of 1951,* by Scottish mountaineer W.H. Murrayhis.

Practice One: Express your love daily with *Affection* and *Appreciation*

Affection — Once a day, embrace for a "15 second passionate kiss."

Appreciation — Once a day, express appreciation for your beloved with *affirming words* about a quality you love, or for something he or she does that you *appreciate*.

Affection

The Kiss

In Chapter Three of *Creating an Intimate Marriage*, author Jim Burns presents a plan for keeping intimate connection alive in your marriage. He says,

> "Daily passionate kissing keeps the fire burning. This is not about sex; it's about intimacy. A passionate kiss before you leave for work leaves a fresh aroma of feelings throughout the day. A passionate kiss when you see each other after a long day apart may be more intimate than anything else you could do to keep the romantic fires burning … passionate kissing, even for just fifteen seconds, releases feelings about each other that say *I love you; I want to be with you; you are special to me*."

Even after 53 years together his words are a "yes" for us. We know that affection and nurturing touch are lifelong needs. The warmth and sensual enjoyment of our passionate kisses enhance our openness to all the expressions of affection we need and desire. We kiss more often. We touch more and hug more. Because the intention of our kiss is intimacy and not a sexual overture, we can, in the moment, freely give and freely receive the full enjoyment of our daily passionate embrace.

Dr. Burns adds that "sex is not an event; it is about creating a positive, romantic, healthy, sexually intimate environment." With a daily habit of affection, when we do come together for sexual intimacy, we enjoy a deeper sense of oneness and pleasure.

In the *Afterglow* of this booklet, pages 44-45, you will find two *nurturing exercises* to guide a conversation about the sexual intimacy in your marriage.

Appreciation

Affirmation

Appreciating your beloved is an essential aspect of a nurtured marriage and a concrete way to "seek each other's best." Yet it is easy to take your beloved's positive attributes for granted and fail to notice them, especially in times of increased stress. Affirmations express appreciation. They create a positive atmosphere that builds self-esteem and reduces conflict. Now that *noticing* and *appreciating* has become a habit for us, it is easy to see what we love about each other and express it. In the noticing, our gratitude for each other grows. In the hearing, we *know* in a deeper way that we are loved and appreciated.

> *"When Metta affirms me, it helps me see my own worth."*
> *"When Milt affirms me, I feel seen, loveable, and valued."*

For those times when it is hard to hold onto our belovedness, reminders can help. Affirming guidelines to follow.

Affirm Your Beloved

Choose a quality from the *Personal Qualities List* on page 13. Take hands and look at each other. Tell your beloved a quality he/she has that you admire or something she/he does that you appreciate. Describe specifically how the quality or action is expressed and a recent time when you *noticed* it. Then tell the impact it has on you — your thoughts and your feelings.*

Examples:
"A quality I love about you is your supportive attitude. I *noticed* it this week during your conversation with our friend needing advice. I was touched by your empathy and validation as you listened to understand his situation. I am proud of you and grateful for your caring heart."

"I liked it this morning when you suddenly stopped what you were doing, came over and hugged me, and told me some things you love about me. I felt warm and assured, and even a bit amorous. I appreciate that spontaneous quality in you and *notice* how deeply I experience your love in moments like this."

*Adapted from *Rewriting Love Stories* by Patricia O'Hanlon Hudson and William Hudson O'Hanlon, W.W. Norton & Company, 1991, for *Marriage Nurturing* by Metta Smith, MA

Receive Words of Affirmation

As pleasant as it is to feel appreciated and loved, many individuals experience an uncomfortable awkwardness when receiving verbal affirmation. We often hear others and ourselves denying, belittling, or dismissing compliments. The affirming exercise is aimed at helping you take in and accept your beloved's gift of appreciation.

While your beloved is sharing an appreciation, your role is to listen and receive without analysis or question. Remember, this is an exercise in receiving love. Try to take in the appreciation like a sponge soaking up water. Notice if you feel resistance, but don't judge it. Thank your beloved for the affirmation.

When you have affirmed each other, share the feelings you experienced while listening to your beloved affirm you.

Adapted from an exercise in *Marriage Enrichment at Home*, Marriage Enrichment Newsletter, October 1987, by David Mace, based on Kathleen and Thomas Hart's book, *The first Two Years of Marriage*.

Personal Qualities

A great friend	Discrete	Open
Active	Enduring	Patient
Adventurous	Enthusiastic	Passionate
Affectionate	Expressive	Persuasive
Alert	Fair	Playful
Assertive	Faithful	Practical
Athletic	Flexible	Proactive
Attentive	Forgiving	Provocative
Available	Generous	Punctual
Bold	Gentle	Reserved
Brave	Graceful	Resourceful
Calm	Grateful	Responsible
Cautious	Helpful	Reverent
Cheerful	Hospitable	Self-controlled
Committed	Humble	Sensitive
Compassionate	Humorous	Sexy
Confident	Imaginative	Sincere
Considerate	Intelligent	Supportive
Content	Intuitive	Tenacious
Coordinated	Joyful	Thorough
Courageous	Kind	Thoughtful
Creative	Lighthearted	Tolerant
Curious	Loving	Trusting
Decisive	Loyal	Truthful
Deferential	Meek	Virtuous
Dependable	Mellow	Vulnerable
Determined	Merry	Warm
Devoted	Mysterious	Winsome
Diligent	Nurturing	Wise
Discerning	Optimistic	Witty
Daring	Organized	Zany

It is impossible to overemphasize the immense need human beings have to be really listened to, to be taken seriously, to be understood … No one can develop fully in this world without feeling understood by at least one person.

Paul Tournier, *To Understand Each Other*

Practice Two: Maintain connection with a *Daily Check-in.*

Connect with each other — Set aside 15 minutes each day to connect and confide in one another about the big and little things happening in your life.

Connect with God together — We invite using your 15 minutes twice a week to connect with God together through a meditative reading of scripture; listening for His invitation for your marriage.

Connect With Each Other

Daily Temperature Reading
by Lori H Gordon, Ph.D.

Confiding — the ability to reveal yourself fully, honestly and directly — is the lifeblood of intimacy. To live together with satisfaction, couples need clear, regular communication. The great intuitive family therapist Virginia Satir developed a technique for partners and families to maintain an easy flow about the big and little things going on in their lives. I have adopted it. Called the *Daily Temperature Reading*, it is very simple (and works for many other kinds of relationships as well).

Do it daily, perhaps as you sit down to breakfast. At first it will seem artificial — hokey, even. In time you'll evolve your own style. Couples routinely report it is invaluable for staying close — even if they let it slide a day or two when they get busy.

The *Temperature Reading* teaches partners how to listen non-defensively and to talk as a way to give information rather than to stir a reaction. Here are the basics: Sit close, perhaps even knee-to-knee, facing your partner, holding each other's hands. This simple touching creates an atmosphere of acceptance for both.

Appreciation — Take turns expressing appreciation for something your partner has done — and thank each other.

New Information — In the absence of information, assumptions — often false ones — rush in. Tell your partner something ("I'm not looking forward to the monthly planning meeting this morning") to keep contact alive and let your partner in on your mood, your experiences---your life. And then listen to your partner.

Puzzles — Take turns asking each other something you don't understand and your partner can explain: "Why were you so down last night?" Or voice a question about yourself: "I don't know why I got so angry while we were figuring out expenses." You might not find answers, but you will be giving your partner some insight about yourself. Besides, your partner may have insights about your experiences.

Hope — Sharing hopes and dreams is integral to a relationship. Hopes can range from the mundane ("I hope you don't have to work late this weekend.") to grandiose ("I'd really love to spend a month in Europe with you"). But the more the two of you bring dreams into immediate awareness, the more likely you'll find a way to realize them.

Complaint with Request for Change — Without placing blame or being judgmental, cite a specific behavior that bothers you and state the behavior you are asking for instead. "If you're going to be late for dinner tonight, will you please call me? That way the kids and I can make a plan for dinner on our own."

The Daily Temperature Reading is an excerpt from the article, "Intimacy: the Art of Working Out Your Relationships," Psychology today, September/October, 1993. Lori H. Gordon, Ph.D., is founder of PAIRS, (Practical Application of Intimate Relationship Skills)

※ ※ ※

Discussing Complaints: Expressing wants and needs in a way that can be heard takes skill and timing. Although complaints are included in the *Daily Temperature Reading,* apart from a simple request regarding daily routines, we discuss relational issues separate from our daily check-in. This keeps our focus on encouragement.

A sudden expression of complaint can trigger fear-based reactive emotion in the hearer. Without preparation, a sudden feeling of vulnerability can easily occur. Common reactions are defensiveness, criticism, and withdrawal. Research shows most arguments occur in this kind of situation.

If you experience the sudden occurrence of reactive emotion, out of respect for yourself and your beloved, immediately take a time out, attend to your feelings with compassion, and use your breath to bring your physiology back into a calm state. Then resume dialogue. (For specific steps, refer to *Rebalancing Reactive Emotion* in the *Appendix*, page 50.)

The examples below are about making a request to talk about a concern. Notice that the request begins with a statement. This creates a context for the hearer and reduces the chance of defensiveness.

(ex. 1) "I'm concerned how little quality time we have, just for us, with our new schedules. Would you be willing to talk with me about it Wednesday evening after the children are in bed?"

(ex.2) "I'm worried about the reactions we are having to this stressful situation we are in. It's starting to affect our relationship. Would you be willing to talk about some kinds of support that can help us reduce our stress and stay connected through this?

For a more complex issue, we schedule a time to talk when we can be alone, relatively rested and free of stress. We make our purpose to *just listen to each other's perspective with compassion and curiosity.* We include the phrase, "tell me more" and the question, "is there anything else?" That helps us stand in the other's shoes and fully understand their view. Later, when the time is right, we brainstorm possible solutions. Our reward is harmony and teamwork. The exercise, *Practice Listening & Giving Feedback, Appendix,* page 51, provides a model for talking about an issue.

Connect With God Together

Our former pastor, David Rohrer, taught us *Lecteo Divina,* a prayerful way of reading the Bible together. He said,

"Lecteo Divina is an ancient practice within the Christian Church. Historically as Protestants, we have tended to stress the use of our intellects for reading and studying the scriptures. This is a strong and valuable part of our tradition. However, we can also use the Bible as a tool for prayer and a way of listening to God."

Lecteo gives us a way to share our spiritual journey and grow in awareness of Jesus' presence with us. It heightens our attention and deepens our listening. We *hear* God's love more clearly and Jesus' invitation to stand by his Spirit, "just for today." Our love and compassion grows.

Choose a place free of distraction. Assume a comfortable position. Begin with a few moments of *centering prayer. Relax your body. Pay attention to your breathing. Breathe in the life God gives you. When you exhale give over to God everything in you that is imperfect. Through this process we quiet ourselves so we can invite the Holy Spirit to remove barriers to our openness and connection with God.*

- Take turns reading the chosen scripture aloud. During the first reading, listen as if hearing the words for the first time.
- Read the Scripture again. Now listen for a word or phrase that captures your imagination or attention. Share with each other **just the word or phrase** that stands out to you.
- Read the same passage out loud a third time. During the third reading, pay attention to the feeling or emotion that you associate with this word or phrase. Following this reading share **just the feeling or emotion.**
- Read the same passage a fourth time out loud. During this reading, listen for what **God may be saying** to you personally and for your marriage through the word or phrase to which you have responded.
- When the fourth reading is complete, take a few moments to ask: "What is **God's invitation** in this Word for today?" When ready, **share your insight**, keeping the text and your insights in mind.
- If time permits, write in a journal one way you would like to develop your life as a couple. Be thoughtful and prayerful, as you consider God's will for your developing intimate marriage.
- End with a prayer for each other.

Lecteo Divina Scripture Suggestions — feel free to choose your own.

Week One: Psalm 103, 1 Corinthians 13: 4-7, Jeremiah 29: 11-13, Ephesians 3: 16-21
Week Two: Psalm 23, John 2: 1-11, Colossians 1: 9-14, Philippians 4: 4-9
Week Three: Psalm 8, Ephesians 4: 29-32 & 5:1, Psalm 34, Isaiah 40: 28-31
Week Four: John 15: 1-12, Proverbs 3:1-6, Psalm 46, Colossians 1: 24-27

(*Lecteo Divina* instruction printed with permission of David Rohrer. *Centering prayer* instruction printed with permission of Renewal Ministries NW)

Practice Three: Increase intimacy and understanding with weekly *"Couple Nurturing Time."*

Once a week schedule a special one-hour "appointment" for a nurturing conversation that enriches your intimate friendship.

Couple Nurturing Time

Our deeper conversations began during a "Marriage Encounter" weekend during our twelfth year of marriage. It was a meaningful, intimate experience that made us aware of the closeness we longed for. Other marriage retreats and workshops followed. Each time we returned home with a sincere desire to hold on to our renewed sense of closeness. Yet each time our intention quickly faded when we resumed our family and work responsibilities.

Fifteen years later we were introduced to a nurturing exercise, created by Pastor Steve Hayner for couples preparing for marriage called, *Growing Through Our Differences.* The twenty-five topics with questions for dialogue helped us begin sharing ourselves more authentically, heart to heart.

We were very hungry. This time, our intention moved from a longing to a weekly goal. For two years, over Saturday breakfast at a local restaurant, we took turns choosing a topic for discussion. With this weekly hour *just for us*, we began our *marriage nurturing* journey. A copy of *Growing Through Our Differences* is in the *Afterglow,* page 39.

Couple Nurturing Conversations

We have chosen four *marriage nurturing exercises* for your weekly, nurturing appointment. These exercises have strengthened our foundation of loving support and enriched our intimate marriage path. Some couples use the exercises as conversation starters. Others complete them separately and then share their answers. You will find what works best for you. We encourage you to take turns initiating *couple nurturing time* and begin each conversation with appreciation.

Week 1:   Love Then and Now or Marriage Nurturing Check-up

Week 2:   I Feel Loved When & Little Love Gifts

Week 3:   Expectations Inventory

Week 4:   It's a Matter of Time

Week One

Love Then and Now

Respond to the following prompts individually, and then discuss your responses with your beloved.

1. Take turns describing your experience of meeting and "falling in love."

2. What qualities in the other did you most admire while you were dating? What are some qualities you admire today?

3. In your first year of marriage, what attitudes and actions helped you sustain your romantic love? (Example: touch, affection, attention, appreciation, romantic date nights, emotional and physical intimacy)

4. What qualities in each of you helped you begin developing a bond of intimate connection and emotional closeness in your first year together? (Examples: commitment, quality time and attention, sharing hopes and dreams, sexual intimacy, mutual support, validation, appreciation and affection)

5. How are you continuing to develop the physical and sexual intimacy in your relationship? What challenges your ongoing development?

6. What has been an unexpected joyful surprise in your marriage?

Adapted for *Marriage Nurturing* from the resource files of the Association for Couples in Marriage Enrichment.

Week One Alternative

Marriage Nurturing Check-up

Annual checkups are good for our cars and our health; they are also good for our marriages! Complete the check-up independently and then share your answers with your beloved. Begin your conversation with an affirmation.

"Something I appreciate about you is_____. A time recently that I have seen it is_____."

1. What are the qualities that I appreciate about our marriage relationship?

2. What factors stand out that make our relationship good right now?

3. What activities are nurturing our relationship at this time? (Examples: expressing affection and appreciation, regular check-ins, prayer, "couple time" for deeper conversations, date night and other activities for enjoyment)

4. What challenges have we faced this past year? (Individually / as a couple)

5. What has most helped us meet the challenges? (Individually / as a couple)

6. Do we have current challenges? If so, how are we addressing them? What are some specific ways we can support each other at this time? Do we need support beyond ourselves: for example a mentor couple, a pastor or a counselor?

7. Looking ahead, what shall we do more of? less of? or, add for our ongoing satisfaction and enjoyment?

Adapted from *The Annual Check-up* exercise, from the resource files of the Association for Couples in Marriage Enrichment, now Better Marriages.

Week Two

Many of us have heard the phrase, "love is a verb." Love is something we do more than something we say. In his book, *The 5 Love Languages*: *The Secret to Love That Lasts*, Gary Chapman goes a step further. He says that the way we express our love is important; that to be meaningful, love must be felt at an emotional level that resonates with the receiver.

Chapman's metaphor of "love languages" is used to describe the various ways that people experience emotional love. It helped us understand our own natural preferences for giving and receiving love. We now appreciate the necessity for learning each other's primary love language so we can be good communicators of love.

We hope you will read *The 5 Love Languages* and discover together what your "primary love language" is. You may also want to visit www.5lovelanguages.com. Perhaps you will discover, as we did, that your languages are different. Now that we know how to give our gifts of love in ways that heighten the other's experience of being loved, we can feel our belovedness more fully and know our love is secure.

Without this knowledge, Chapman says, "… the love you offer will most likely be the kind you want to receive and not what the other needs." The *I Feel Loved When* and *Little Love Gifts* exercises will give you ideas for expressing your love in ways that touch your beloved's heart.

I Feel Loved When….

Feeling loved and cared for by one special person is a gift and a pleasure. At the same time, the romantic myth is "If he (she) really loved me, he (she) would know what I want." Yet as much as we wish it were true, it is an unrealistic expectation to think that your beloved can "just naturally know" what helps you feel especially loved.

The following exercise gives you an opportunity to share directly with your beloved what gives you a *heart-felt* sense of being loved.

Complete the following sentence with at least five actions or behaviors your mate has done (at any time) that have helped you feel loved or that you have especially appreciated. Take turns telling each other what you have chosen.

I feel loved when … (or) I appreciate it when you …

1.

2.

3.

4.

5.

6.

7.

8.

9.

10.

Which of these behaviors could you easily repeat more frequently? Which ones would you also be willing to do even if they seem harder?

Adapted from exercise in "Marriage Enrichment at Home," Marriage Enrichment Newsletter, Feb., 1989. From resource files of the Association for Couples in Marriage Enrichment (A.C.M.E).

Little Love Gifts

Acts of kindness help us give and receive love in tangible ways. Offering our gifts of love in ways that are meaningful to each other keeps our love alive and vibrant. Surprise your beloved once a week with an act of kindness.

Circle three love gifts that you know give you a *heart-felt* emotional experience of love. Share something about the activities that makes them especially meaningful to you.

- Invite me on a walk, bike ride or some other outdoor activity.
- Hug me until I say stop.
- Prepare a romantic dinner ~ candles, music, conversation about hopes and dreams, etc.
- Make breakfast.
- Bring me flowers.
- Give me a foot massage.
- Invite me to dance to our favorite music.
- Take me to a ballgame.
- Call forth my strengths.
- Send me a love note.
- Fold my laundry.
- Kiss me or tell me you love me when I least expect it.
- Arrange a surprise weekend getaway.
- Help me wash my car.
- Express appreciation for something I have done.
- Other ways:
- _____
- _____
- _____

Exchange lists so you can choose three to give as "little love gifts" this week.

Week Three

Expectation Inventory

Leaving expectations unspoken can lead to misunderstandings and disappointment. We all have ideas about what *will or should* be included in the various aspects of our marriage relationship; what is true individually and what is true in a thriving intimate couple relationship.

By clarifying your expectations for your relationship and sharing them with your beloved, you can work toward agreement about how you will live together in harmony and mutual satisfaction. Work on the inventory separately.

Be specific. Include such things as qualities, attitudes, actions and activities. When finished, come together to compare and explore your answers.

1. My expectations about our time together, alone, with friends and family are …

2. Define friendship with my beloved as …

3. For personal growth I picture …

4. I define intimacy as …

5. For developing relational closeness I picture …

6. To me, quality time includes …

7. To me, romance includes …

8. Sexual pleasure for me includes …

9. I feel supported by my beloved when …

10. Regarding money, my beliefs and ideas include … (values, decision making, final say, budgeting, hopes and dreams)

11. Regarding my work I expect … (values, strengths, aptitudes, likes, dislikes, etc.)

12. Other topics for dialogue are …

Week Four

It's a Matter of Time

Giving your beloved your full attention is a gift of love. In his book, *The Road Less Traveled*, Scott Peck makes this stunning statement: "The principal form that the work of love takes is attention."

Attention says, "I want to know you." It says, "I'm interested in you." "I care about what you care about." With adequate affirming attention, we grow into more of who we are.

Peck also says, "By far, the most common and important way we can exercise our attention is by listening." True listening, according to him, is "total concentration on the other." It requires "the discipline of bracketing, or the temporary setting aside of one's own prejudices and desires to experience the speaker's world from the inside. It requires courage, consistency and patience."

Listening can only occur, he says, "when time is set aside for listening and the conditions are supportive of it."

As essential as quality time together is for staying connected, for many of us today with over overcommitted lives, creating space just to know and nurture each other can seem daunting. *It's a Matter of Time* questions on the next page can help you evaluate your how time is allocated now. With this information you will be able to imagine and create an hour during the week for deepening your intimate friendship and connection.

Decide on a time when you can be alone, rested and relatively free of stress to answer the questions. Share your answers.

It's a Matter of Time Questions

1. How would you define quality time and what it means to you?

2. List the times you are together during a typical week, estimating how much time is spent on each activity.

3. Rate the quality of each activity you listed, using a scale from 1 (low) to 10 (high).

4. Identify some things that you believe get in the way of quality couple time each week. Identify specific things you have done together in the past to create satisfying times together. How might these actions help you create a space for couple nurturing time during the week?

5. Describe what a meaningful hour would look like to you.

6. Share what could help you commit to a "special time just for us" each week, after the 30-day practice ends. (See the *Afterglow,* page 33-45, for ideas.)

7. Share what could help you keep it going.

8. With mutual agreement, set a time to plan an hour "couple nurturing time" and try it out for two or three weeks. Evaluate what worked and what didn't and make adjustments.

Adapted from *It's a Matter of Time*, Association for Couples for Marriage Enrichment (A.C.M.E.), Now, *Better Marriages*.

Finale — Share and Celebrate

Consider a group celebration — Share the results of your 30-day practice with the other *brave couples*.

Plan a special date night — Celebrate with your beloved.

Share and Celebrate

Plan a Group Celebration

Share with the other *brave couples* or with family and friends what you discovered. Share what you will take with you for ongoing connection, intimacy, and hope for a great marriage through all the seasons of life. Share what you have planned for a special Date Night to celebrate your 30-day marriage nurturing practice.

Prepare for Group Celebration

Review and reflect on the thirty days of marriage nurturing together or separately and compare your answers.

- What have you discovered from putting your marriage first for thirty days?

- What was most meaningful for you and why?

- What do you hope you will carry forward?

- What would you like to share with the other *brave couples*?

- Who else do you want to share your discoveries with?

Plan Your "Date Night" Celebration

- Describe what a "special date night" would look like to you.

- Make a plan.

- Choose the time and place.

- Enjoy — Don't forget to kiss.

Afterglow

Resources for Future Marriage Nurturing

Taking Off and Putting On
Considering the Spirituality of Marriage

Marriage Nurturing Vision Exercise

Growing Through Our Differences

Ten Principles of a Good Sexual Relationship

Sharing Private Thoughts & Feelings about Sex

(This essay is an introduction to University Presbyterian Church's "Life Together: Preparing for Marriage" class. Please read Genesis 2:18-25 and Colossians 3:12-17 before you read this essay.)

Taking Off and Putting On
Considering the Spirituality of Marriage

By Pastor David Rohrer

Part of what it means to be human is our capacity to give and receive love, and the exercise of this capacity shapes much of our lives. We are all on a quest for love. It is a relentless search that fuels our decisions and motivates our behavior. Yet one of the great ironies in our search is that we are searching for something that we hope will find us. What we want is to be hit by cupid's arrow. We want to fall in love, stumble upon it—be overwhelmed by it; for there is no feeling that can match this feeling of being consumed by passion for our beloved and by our beloved's passion for us.

This is the kind of love that initiates most romantic relationships. We fall into a pit of passion and we are so overwhelmed by the good feeling of it that we are virtually unaware of how we got here.

Yet there is another kind of love that sustains a relationship over years. This is the choice to love, the love of a covenant. To be in a loving covenant relationship with another is to choose to seek the other's best. It is to give oneself to the work of helping to create an environment in which we can grow in intimacy with our beloved. It is to declare our vow that we will be here for that person through good and bad, thick and thin.

It is God who teaches us about this covenant love, and he does so by loving us in this way. God chooses to love us, chooses to stay in relationship with us, chooses to seek our best. By this faithfulness he builds intimacy with us; he creates an environment of safety and trust. He fosters an environment that is brimming over with grace and gratitude where we are free to reveal ourselves to him and free to grow into all that he intends for us to be.

When a man and a woman marry, they declare their choice to enter into such a covenant relationship. They choose to commit themselves to a life of faithfulness and trust, and as a result of this choice, they create an environment of safety and freedom.

As you stand on the threshold of declaring this choice, it is helpful to know a bit about the nature of this covenant commitment. Two passages from the Bible give us some insight into what this covenant looks like. In Genesis 2:18-25 and Colossians 3:12-17 we see that creating the context of covenant love is both about taking something off and putting something on. It is about shedding what stands in the way of intimacy and putting on the qualities that build an environment of faithfulness and trust.

In the Genesis passage we learn something about how a covenant involves shedding the things that prevent union with one another. As a remedy for loneliness and isolation God creates the woman to be with the man. She is both similar to him and different from him. She is declared by God to be a helper who is his partner. And when God brings her to the man, the man proclaims her to be "bone of my bone and flesh of my flesh." She is one who is like him. She is a power equal unto him.

But she is also different from him. She is woman. Taken out of him and yet separate from him. And in this difference each will face the challenge of having to make space for the other. Each will have to give something up for the other.

Here is one of the first challenges of marriage, which is also one of the greatest gifts of marriage. We cannot come together without giving something up. We must each open up some kind of space in ourselves for our spouse. We must allow our world to be invaded by our spouse and thus open ourselves to the possibility of being challenged by him or her. To come together we have to shed what might keep us apart. The prerogatives of individualism must give way to a mutual dedication to seek the other's best. Each partner has a gift to give to the other and that gift can only be given when the other chooses to open up space in him/herself in order to receive it.

According to the writer of Genesis, something else must be shed as well. We must leave one family in order to start a new one. The writer says, "... a man leaves his father and his mother and clings to his wife." This covenant union of marriage can only survive if we shed other relationships that might divert our attention or stand in our way. The strong marital covenant is the one that shows respect for our families of origin, but does not allow this family to overly influence our choices and direction. We must take off an old identity in order to make space for a new one. While we will never stop being the children of our parents, marriage gives us the opportunity to create a new family.

The passage ends with a comment about the nature of the relationship between the man and the woman: "And the man and the woman were both naked and were not ashamed." In order for there to be union, there must be nakedness. The strong marriage covenant is one where each person feels the freedom to be vulnerable and real with the other. The masks must come off; the barriers to intimacy must come down. Thus the strong covenant relationship is the one that allows us to undress: to reveal who we are to the other and to allow the other to reveal him/herself to us.

The covenant of marriage is about taking something off. But it is also about putting something on. We must put on the things that nurture and build up one another. We must build an environment where nakedness and vulnerability are possible because they are encouraged and protected.

St. Paul gives us an idea as to what ingredients go into the making of such an environment in Colossians 3:12-17. He begins with the admonition, "... clothe yourselves with compassion, kindness, humility, meekness and patience." In other words, put on the qualities that will enable you to extend yourself for the sake of the other. Put on the things that will help you to make room for the other. Compassion, kindness, humility, meekness, and patience are the qualities that promote gentleness in a marriage. They are the tools that help a couple to negotiate conflicts and build intimacy. They are the qualities that help to remind you of your primary mission of knowing and encouraging one another. Apart from their presence, it is almost impossible to create a context in which covenant love can grow.

However, compassion, kindness, humility, meekness and patience will not always be present. When they aren't, the chances are good that you will hurt one another. Thus it is necessary to put on another quality as well. It is important that you know how to put on forgiveness.

Forgiveness is the willingness to step back and see the bigger picture. It is the choice to remind yourself that there is something bigger than the hurt that your partner caused. It is the willingness to believe that there is something bigger than the wedge that is coming between you, something more enduring than the source of your conflict. In effect, to forgive your partner is to affirm that you are both committed to the same big goal of seeking the other's best, and that you want to get on with the business of doing just that.

Forgiveness is something that we learn from God. St. Paul tells us to "let the peace of Christ rule in [our] hearts" and to "let the word of Christ dwell in [us] richly." This is the key to learning how to forgive. When we learn what it means to be forgiven by God, we learn how to forgive one another. The One who loved us teaches us about the nature of true love. Christ sought us out, he made space for us, he forgave us, he wants what is best for us. To let his peace and his word dwell in us allows us to take in the resources that enable us to learn to love one another.

The covenant of marriage is nurtured by taking something off and putting something on. We must remove those things that stand in the way of intimacy and put on the things that promote it. But as we go about this task of taking off and putting on, we need to know that we do not embark on this journey alone. There is One who has gone before us, One who is with us now, one who will never leave us, who will hold onto us and support even when we have no energy to support one another.

So as Paul says, "Whatever you do in word and deed, do everything in the name of the Lord Jesus, giving thanks to God the Father through him." Place this Lord of love and life at the center of your life, and thus the center of your marriage, and you will learn how to love one another. Let him hold onto you and so equip you with the resources you need to build a lasting and fulfilling life together.

Marriage Nurturing Vision

Soon after my husband and I rededicated our marriage on our 35th anniversary, we read *Getting The Love You Want,* by Harville Hendrix. We gained insight and learned practical ways to enhance our relationship. The last chapter is about creating a vision and its value for "getting the love you want."

His "Relationship Vision" exercise has been invaluable to our ongoing journey of *intimate companionship*. We included specific behaviors that strengthen our bond while increasing our marital satisfaction and enjoyment. Examples from our personal Relationship Vision: *We are devoted to our marriage ~ We affirm each other daily ~ We share our hopes, dreams, needs and wants.* Periodically, we review our vision and notice without judgment areas that may need attention.

The following exercise is used with permission from Harville Hendrix, Ph.D.

Your Relationship Vision Exercise

Time: Approximately 60 minutes.
Purpose*:* This exercise will help you see the potential in your relationship.
Comments: Do this exercise together.

Directions
1. Take out two sheets of paper, one for each of you. Working separately, write a series of short sentences that describe your personal vision of a deeply satisfying love relationship. Include qualities you already have that you want to keep and qualities you wish you had. For marriage nurturing also include items that will nurture your emotional and spiritual connection. Write each sentence in the present tense, as if it were already happening. For example: "We have fun together." "We have great sex." "We are affectionate with each other." Make all your items positive statements. Write "we settle our differences peacefully" rather than "we don't fight."

2. Share your sentences. Note the items that you have in common and underline them. (It doesn't matter if you have used different words, as long as the general idea is the same.) If your partner has written sentences that you agree with but did not think of yourself, add them to your list. For the moment, ignore items that are not shared.

3. Now turn to your own expanded list and rank each sentence (including the ones that are *not* shared) with a number from 1 to 5 according to its importance to you, with 1 indicating "very important" and 5 indicating "not so important."

4. Circle the two items that are most important to you.

5. Put a check mark by those items that you both agree would be difficult to achieve.

6. Now work *together* to design a relationship (nurturing) vision similar to the example below; start with the items that you both agree are most important. At the bottom of the list, write items that are relatively unimportant. If you have items that are a source of conflict between you, see if you can come up with a compromise statement that satisfies both of you. If not, leave the item in your combined list.

7. Post this list where you can see it daily. Once a week, at the beginning of your work sessions, read it aloud to each other.

Our Relationship Vision

Bill		Jenny
1	We have fun together.	1
1	We settle our differences peacefully.	1
1	We have satisfying and beautiful sex.	1
1	We are healthy and physically active.	1
1	We communicate easily and openly.	1
1	We worship together.	1
1	We are each other's best friend.	1
1	We have secure and happy children.	1
2	We trust each other.	1
1	We are sexually faithful.	1
2	We both have satisfying careers.	2
2	We work well together as parents.	2
2	We meet each other's deepest needs.	2
3	We have daily private time.	4
3	We feel safe with each other.	2
3	We are financially secure.	4
4	We live close to our parents.	5
5	We have similar political views	3

Growing Through Our Differences
Some Questions for a Maturing Relationship
Steve and Sharon Hayner

The following questions are designed to help think through your relationship more clearly and to facilitate deeper communication. This is NOT a checklist to measure compatibility or your readiness for marriage. Think about your relationship individually in light of the following categories. Note areas of particular strength or weakness. How are the two of you similar? How are you different? How do you deal with your differences? Make notes in the margin, particularly about those areas that are difficult to talk about.

---

1. **COMPANIONABILITY/SHARING**

    Real love wants to share, give, reach out, care. How do I want the very best for this person? What qualities of a good friendship are part of our relationship? When am I willing to give up my own rights for the sake of the other? How do I know that I love the other even when I don't feel it? When do I feel needed by my beloved?

2. **COMMUNICATION**

    Can we share meaningfully? Do we understand each other in our communication? Do we enjoy talking about a variety of things? Do we listen to each other effectively? How deep is our conversation? ... reporting facts? ... relating ideas, judgments? ... sharing feelings? ... risking total honesty? What topics do we avoid in our communication?

3. **RESPECT**

    Are we able to respect each other in a variety of situations? Am I proud of this person? ... in what areas? Are there areas about which I am not very proud? Are there any characteristics that I consistently don't want to talk about with my friends and/or family?

4. **LEADERSHIP/DECISION-MAKING**

    How do we make decisions? Are we content with the patterns that have developed? Are we able to submit to one another? Are there areas where I wish that the other would lead more, or take more responsibility/initiative? Are there times when I feel "squeezed out" or ignored? How do we view roles and responsibilities in marriage?

5. **VIEW OF MARRIAGE**

    How do we view the relationship of marriage? What do we want our marriage to look like? What were my expectations for marriage? What areas are most important to each of us in marriage? What do I consider to be important elements/goals which will help a marriage to grow? Is divorce ever justified? If so, under what circumstances?

6. **DEALING WITH CONFLICT**

    No close relationship can be achieved and maintained in any other way than by resolving the conflict that it inevitably produces. Are we able to quarrel productively? What is each of our patterns when we fight? Are we able to forgive one another? Does either of us tend to hold grudges? Have I built any pockets of bitterness in our relationship?

7. **INTERESTS**

    What interests do we share? How enthusiastic am I about the other's interests? Where do our interests diverge? Have we developed any new interests together?

8. **EMOTIONS**

    Do we share our feelings with each other? How would we describe each other's temperament? How would I describe mine? Do we build each other emotionally? How do I feel emotionally after a time together? Do I feel at ease when we are together or under a strain?

9. **ENJOYMENT/RECREATION**

    Do we enjoy each other's company without constant physical expression? Do we have fun together? How much are we able to laugh together? What helps the other to relax? What helps me to relax? How are we similar or different in this area?

10. **TRUST/CONSISTENCY**

    Do I trust the other person to be with other friends? Do I trust our relationship in the context of others? Can I trust the other to tell the truth? Does the other person demonstrate the same personal characteristics when we are apart as when we are together?

11. **HABITS**

    Are we able to accept each other's habits? Are there significant areas of behavior that bother me about the other? Which of my habits are most irritating? In which areas have we most often found ourselves promising to change? Where have we been disappointed in each other?

12. LIFE-STYLE/LIFE GOALS

How well do we understand each other's goals and dreams? Which goals do we share? How fully can I describe what kind of life the other person wants to have 3-5 years from now? How do I see myself fitting into that picture? What do we each want out of our marriage? What values do we each consider to be important in life-style decisions? How do we each reflect our priorities in the use of time and money?

13. INTELLECTUAL INTERESTS

Where do our mental interests and capabilities overlap? What do I like to think about? Where do I wish that I knew more about the other person's intellectual world? How much do I feel the other knows about this area of my life?

14. VOCATIONAL UNDERSTANDING

How do I currently feel about my vocation/career? How do our vocations affect our relationship? What do I wish I knew/understood better about the other's vocation/career? How do our long-term goals mesh? How do they differ?

15. FAMILY

When we marry, we don't just marry a person, but rather a whole family! What have we learned about each other's family? What have I learned about my own recently? How do I fit into the other's family? How does the other fit into my family? What are the most striking characteristics of each of our family backgrounds? What do we each think is important in family life?

16. FRIENDS

What do we each appreciate in friends? Does the other person like my friends? Do I like his/her friends? What role do our friends play in our life together? How do our friendships affect our relationship? How are we able to share our relationship and time together with others?

17. CHILDREN

How do I feel about children? How does the other person feel? What comes to mind when I think about having children? How have we differed in our ways of handling children?

18. HEALTH

How do I cope with illness in myself and in others? How have health-related issues in our lives impacted our marriage? What life patterns related to physical health are important to each of us? What are our individual approaches to dealing with health, medical treatment, and our bodies in general?

19. CHANGE

How well do I handle unfulfilled expectations? What is the hardest part about change for me? How does my approach to change differ from that of the other person? How would I rank each of us on an "adventure and risk" scale?

20. MONEY

What does money represent in my life? ...security? ...identity? ...useful tool? How do I make decisions about money? How is my approach different from that of the other person? Are we "spenders" or "savers"? Which of us worries more about money? How big an issue has money been in our relationship thus far? How do we each approach financial planning?

21. ROMANCE

What areas do I find most attractive in the other? What effect has our romance had on each of our personalities? What does distance (or long separation) do to our relationship? How do I wish that the other person would express love to me? How do I most often express love? What would we each describe as "a romantic moment"? How do we nurture our romance?

22. SEXUALITY

How big a part does my sexuality play in who I am? What have I learned about sexuality in our relationship? How important is sex to the other person? How do our attitudes about sex differ? What do I wish were different about our sexual behavior? How comfortable are we in talking about this area?

23. SPIRITUAL GROWTH

What are the dynamics of my life with Christ right now? In our relationship, what common spiritual experiences, understandings, backgrounds and/or commitments do we share? How are we different in our spiritual journeys and dynamics? What do I contribute to the other's life with Christ? What does the other contribute to my walk? How do I wish we functioned differently in this area of our life together?

24. SERVING OTHERS

Are there areas of service beyond our relationship about which I have strong feelings? What are the other person's primary areas of service? How do we help each other to care for others? What common goals do we share beyond our relationship? In what areas of our stewardship are each of us strongest and weakest: time, talents, skills, care, money, etc.?

25. ENDURANCE/COMMITMENT

How long have we known each other? Under what circumstances have we grown/deepened in our understanding of one another? How would I describe my commitment to our relationship? In what ways do I think the other person's commitment is different from mine? What is the hardest trial that we have endured together? What did I learn about the other through that time?

Used with permission from the late Pastor Steve Hayner and his wife Sharon Hayner. *Growing Through Our Differences* was originally created by Pastor Hayner for couples preparing for marriage who were associated with University Ministries, known as The Inn, at University Presbyterian Church, Seattle Washington.

Ten Basic Principles of a Good Sexual Relationship

Read the list of principles listed below together and use them as a springboard for talking about your sexual relationship. Make your goal to increase your sense of comfort in discussing lovemaking with your beloved in order to gain awareness of satisfaction or dissatisfaction in your sexual relationship.

1. The goal of sexual lovemaking is giving and receiving love and pleasure. This is the only objective and says nothing about climax or orgasm. Do not ask for an orgasm.

2. Giving is pleasurable and can be enjoyed but should be on a non-demand basis. Ask only that your partner receive your gift.

3. Learn to receive pleasure without feeling obligated to give. By enjoying the gift of your partner you are giving pleasure.

4. Sex is a long continuum of activity and not just intercourse. Sexuality and sensuality are intimately related. Sensuality includes touching, smelling, tasting, hearing and seeing.

5. Sex is an interaction requiring clear communication and willing cooperation. Hear what your partner says without feeling criticized.

6. Learn to say "yes" instead of "no". Give alternatives. Break the rejection cycle. Say "yes" to the relationship and "no" to specific behaviors.

7. More enjoyable sex is better than increased quantity of sex. Enjoyable activity is self-reinforcing.

8. Sex should be fun and not work. Enjoyable sex requires interesting and interested partners.

9. Closeness may, at times, be too much, and either partner may need distance. It is important to learn to ask for distance without showing abandonment. Give reassurance to your beloved that you will return.

10. Go slowly, give plenty of reassurance as needed.

Adapted from material from the Division of Community and Social Psychiatry, University of Texas Medical Branch.

Sharing Private Thoughts & Feelings about Sex

Physical expressions of love, including sex are important for marital satisfaction. Gender difference, sexual desire variables, and other individual factors make teaching each other about your sexual needs and desires essential. This exercise will help you talk heart-to-heart about your sexual relationship.

In my family of origin I learned the following about sex …

My beliefs and desires for our sexual relationship now are …

Kinds of affection that I love are …

Things that create romance for me are … or, I feel romantic when …

Some ways you make love with me that I love are …

To get ready for making love with you I need …

A way for you to initiate sex that turns me on is …

Some other things that turn me on sexually are …

Something else I enjoy is …

How can I tell you what I desire while we are making love and not disturb our intimacy?

How can I let you know I am too tired or stressed for lovemaking that would help you not personalize it?

When I need to turn you down, I feel …

When you need to turn me down, I feel …

Something new I would like to try in our lovemaking is …

Adapted from Marriage Enrichment exercise from the resource files of Association for Couples for Marriage Enrichment, A.C.M.E., now, Better Marriages.

Therefore, as God's chosen people, holy and dearly loved,
Clothe yourselves with compassion, kindness, humility, gentleness and patience.
Bear with each other and forgive one another. Forgive as the Lord forgave you.
And over all these virtues put on love, which binds them all together in perfect unity.

1 Corinthians 13:13

Appendix

Ground Rules for Group Support

Rebalancing Reactive Emotions

Practice Listening & Giving Feedback

Acknowledgements

References

Ground Rules for Group Support

In order for your group to become a safe place for personal interactions, it is important to agree on some ground rules:

Confidentiality
It is a privilege and a responsibility to share our lives with one another in an environment of trust, respect, and confidence. Confidentiality is essential to the group process. What is shared in this group stays in this group.

Sharing Experiences
Our goal is to share from our own marriage experiences in order to reduce isolation, and to support and encourage one another. To accomplish this here, we ask you to avoid intellectualizing, diagnosing, analyzing and giving advice.

Participation is Voluntary
Each person decides his or her level of participation. If you decide not to participate in an exercise or dialogue, that is all right as long as you avoid interfering with those who are participating.

This includes times when sharing is structured to move from person to person around the circle. "I pass on this one," is all that is needed to indicate that you'd rather not share. It is also important that everyone is given an opportunity to share. Therefore, we ask that you give others a chance to speak before sharing a second time.

Couple Consensus
When you talk about your marriage you are also sharing things about your spouse. Please confirm with your beloved before sharing information about the two of you as a couple. This protects your confidentiality as a couple and avoids strife.

Also, speaking for others is common in our culture. In BRAVE COUPLES' exercises we want you to practice speaking for yourself. To do this we ask you to refrain from talking about your beloved by focusing on your own experience and using "I" statements.

Concerns Come First

A concern is a worry or preoccupation that interferes with a person's full participation within the group (for example, an unexpected family illness or job change). When someone has a concern, it will take precedence within the group. The individual needs only to say, "I have a concern," and the group action will stop to allow that person to share the concern and ask for what they need from the group.

Emotions

Making changes sometimes triggers uncomfortable emotions. They can lead to conflict. If you need help getting through it, we hope you will bring your concern to your group of *brave couples* for encouragement, support, and prayer.

Timeliness

A group works best if all are present when the session begins. Be committed to start and finish on time. Please try to arrive a few minutes early.

Prayer

In the early 1970's my husband and I had an opportunity to attend a couples retreat about prayer. It was led by Armin Gesswein, founder and director of Revival Prayer Fellowship, who is also an Associate Evangelist for the Billy Graham Evangelistic Association. We were young in our faith and Mr. Gesswein helped us understand that Jesus, above all else, wants us to know that God loves and cares for us.

He talked about Jesus extending his *"resurrection power* toward those who believe." He explained that Jesus joins us through the power of the Holy Spirit when we pray together "in His name."

Jesus' promise in Matthew 18:19 took on new meaning.

> *Again, I tell you that if two of you on earth agree about anything you ask for, it will be done for you by my Father in heaven. For where two or three come together in my name, there am I with them."*

Finally, Mr. Gesswein told us that when we are joined as *one* in Christ, our ability to agree in prayer may be stronger than in any other relationship. In our *oneness,* we could also have great assurance of Jesus hearing and answering our prayers. That retreat marked the beginning of our prayer life together.

Rebalancing Reactive Emotions

1. Recognize that you feel reactive, i.e., defensive, critical, put downs, flooded. Acknowledge it and if necessary, take a break from the discussion to calm your emotion.

2. Consciously take in a slow deep breath with your mouth closed; breathe in from the diaphragm. Hold it to the count of five. As you exhale completely, let your jaw, tongue and shoulders go limp. Relax.
    a. This sends more oxygen to your brain. It helps you turn off the *reactive mode* of your brain and return to the *responsive mode*, the "baseline condition of your brain that is aware, even-keeled, contented, benign and integrated."
    b. Once back in the *responsive mode*, you have access again to your frontal lobe's reasoning capacity for coping creatively and effectively with a difficult situation.

3. Continue breathing into your belly and extend compassion to your reactive feelings. Use "self-soothing" thoughts and words to calm your distress like, "quiet mind, calm body," "I'm okay," "We can work through this."

4. When your physiology has returned to normal, resume your dialogue about the situation that triggered your reaction. In a more relaxed state, you are better able to access your loving connection with your beloved and talk about what you felt, need, and want, in relation to the triggering event.

Rick Hanson, PhD., "Your Wonderful Brain", 2007

Practice Listening & Giving Feedback

This is a listening exercise. Choose a topic that is important to you. For practice choose a topic that is not controversial or carries a relational component. During the exercise each person will have a turn being the "talker" and the "listener."

Role of the Talker: Describe your chosen topic and talk about your thoughts, feelings, and desires regarding the topic; practice speaking with "I" statements; avoid "You" statements.

Role of the Listener: Temporarily put aside your own thoughts and feelings about the topic so you can focus your energy on gaining a complete understanding of your beloved's view of the topic.

The Talker will discuss the topic without interruption, questions, or opinions by the listener for an agreed upon length of time. However, depending on the amount of information being shared, the listener may reach a limit to what can be taken in. If this occurs, the concept of "chunking" is helpful— the listener interrupts the talker to summarize what has been heard so far. Following the summary, the talker resumes sharing to completion.

The Listener will then provide feedback by acknowledging the thoughts, feelings, and desires that the talker has expressed.

After the initial feedback, the talker will either confirm that the message was understood or try again to clarify and communicate the message again.

When both are satisfied that the first talker has been correctly heard and understood, switch roles and repeat the process using the same topic.

Adapted from the resource files of the Association for Couples in Marriage Enrichment (A.C.M.E.) www.bettermarriages.com, for *Marriage Nurturing,* by Metta Smith.

References

Burns, Jim, *Creating and Intimate Marriage,* Bethany House Publishers, Bloomington, Minnesota, 2006.

Chapman, Gary, *The Five Love Languages*, Northfield Publishing, Chicago, 1995.

Hendrix, Harville, *Getting The Love You Want*. Harper Perennial, New York, 1988.

Tournier, Paul, *To Understand Each Other*, John Knox Press, Louisville KY, 2004.

Markman, Howard, Scott Stanley & Susan L. Blumburg, *Fighting for Your Marriage,* Jossey-Bass Inc., San Francisco, CA, 1994.

Scriptures' quotations are taken from the HOLY BIBLE, NEW INTERNATIONAL VERSION ®. Copyright © 1973, 1978, 1984 by International Bible Society.

Peck, Scott M., *The Road Less Traveled*, Simon & Schuster, 1978.

Real, Terrance, *The New Rules for Marriage,* Ballantine Books, New York, 2008.

Acknowledgements

With gratitude, I want to acknowledge the participants in our *Marriage Nurturing* classes, who have inspired the creation of BRAVE COUPLES, a condensed version of *Marriage Nurturing* that invites couples to taste its delights and see its value. Their encouragement keeps my dream of a nurtured, intimate marriage for all couples alive and moving forward.

~ For my sweetheart Milt, who loves and encourages me. As lovers and best friends, we have practiced, with many do-overs, learning the steps of our intimate marriage dance. I am grateful for his willingness to keep growing with me through each stage of our life together.

~ For our *Marriage Nurturing Matters* Board, who share our vision of supporting couples in their desire for a life-long thriving marriages — Jon & Lexi Kamrath, Margaret & Erik Giesa, and Dustin & Holly Wood.

~ For Jon Kamrath's willingness and expertise for setting up our *Marriage Nurturing Matters* website and managing its ongoing development (www.marriagenurturing.org).

~ For Bethany Presbyterian Church's shared vision for marriage enrichment, providing support through their Christian Education Committee.

~ For the four other couples on Bethany's Marriage Team, who are working with Milt and me to build a container for marriage education and support — Kurt & Delene Deforest-Dale, Jon & Lexi Kamrath, Josh & Jessica Marion, and Sean & Barbie Kelly.

~ For our daughter, Julie Reinhardt, who has provided encouragement and applied her keen copy editing skills to the project.

~ For my friend, Judith Ryan, who brought her skills and creativity as editor and publisher for BRAVE COUPLES; for her photography which she generously gifted to the project; and for the enjoyment of working together in co-creation.

~ For all the *brave couples*, who by their commitment to intentional marriage nurturing, are creating a new future for themselves, their families and our culture.

Made in the USA
San Bernardino, CA
21 February 2016